Poems with Moxie

Funny Poems & Funny Songs

Poems with Moxie

ISBN: 0-9709569-4-0
ISBN-13: 978-0-9709569-4-1

Sasha —
You've got
MOXIE!
2012

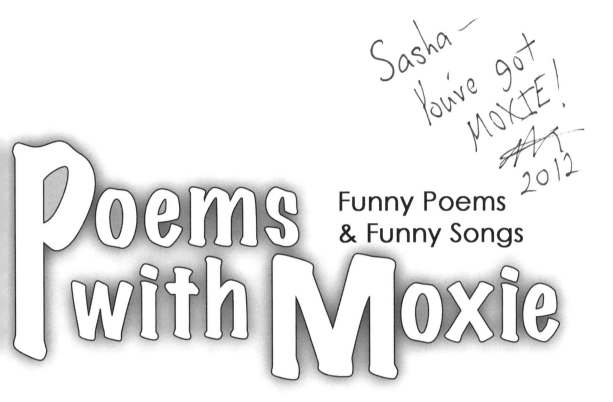

Poems with Moxie

Funny Poems
& Funny Songs

Poems by
Robert Pottle

Illustrations by
Holly Hardwick

 Blue Lobster Press

Blue Bananas

Sing to the tune of "Oh, Susanna"

At school I like to doodle
lots of weird and wacky things,
like goats with capes
and coats for grapes
and phones with wedding rings.

My mind will often drift
just like a big hot air balloon
where chocolate rains
on subway planes
and honey fills the moon.

Blue bananas
are dancing on a stage.
During class I daydream
as I doodle on the page.

And when the class is doing math
I'm drawing all my thoughts
of monkey kings
and worms with wings
that tie themselves in knots.

Blue bananas
are dancing on a stage.
During class I daydream
as I doodle on the page.

My teacher says I spend my life
in worlds that don't exist.
But there's not one
that isn't fun,
so how can I resist?

Blue bananas
are dancing on a stage.
During class I daydream
as I doodle on the page.

The Artist

From drawing blue bananas,
my marker has gone dry.
I'll use my mouth to moisten it
and give another try.

My marker's working better now.
And, wow, I love the taste.
It's surprisingly more flavorful
than crayons, chalk or paste!

Katie starts to giggle.
I ask, "What's wrong with you?"
She points at me, laughs and says,
"Your tongue is colored blue!"

6

My tongue is blue! How cool is that?
I'm artistic, and it shows.
I grab a green. I open it
and color on my nose.

Then with purple, pink, and gray,
yellow, brown, and red,
I color ears and eyes and teeth.
I'm Mrs. Rainbow Head!

Miss Libby looks and throws a fit:
"Why can't you just be good?"
It's hard to be an artist
when you're so misunderstood.

Time Out Limerick #1

I don't mean to be such a pest.
I thought I was doing my best.
When I made the kids laugh
by burping in class
my teacher was not so impressed.

Time Out Limerick #2

I got into trouble again.
All 'cause I used my new pen.
See, art class was boring
till Jen started snoring
and now there's a mustache on Jen.

Time Out Limerick #3

Today I was playing with Ben.
Just cutting some paper, and then,
I cut off his hair
till his head was half bare,
and now I'm in trouble again.

Classroom Dolls

Miss Libby says the dolls look best
   when dressed in pinks and reds.
I think the classroom dolls look best
   when they have no heads.

Super Spy

He has eyes that see through walls,
   and ears that hear my thoughts.
He watches me 'bout every day;
   it ties my gut in knots.
I'd like to take his spying head
   and shove it in a pail,
'cause no one likes — especially me
   the classroom tattle-tale.

First Day of Kindergarten

Today was it. I went to school.
It was fun and kinda cool.
We did the hokey-pokey dance.
Peter cried — he wet his pants.
Miss Libby said to make a line.
I got paper. I drew mine.
But all the kids were in a row.
Miss Libby said, "Come on, let's go."
I sang and drew and had some fun.
I've gone to school, and now I'm
done.

Huh?
What did you say?
I've got to go another day?
I am not done this afternoon?
I've got to go until mid-June!
I thought today I was all done.
I guess today was just day one.

How to Avoid the
Underwear-Eating Toilet Monster

Down below the toilet seat
lives a mean ferocious beast.
He likes to give young kids a scare
then eat their pants and underwear.

This beast's a creature of the night
because he's scared to death of light.
So, when you have to go at night,
don't forget — turn on the light!

Where, Oh, Where Have My Underwear Gone?

Sing to the tune of "Where, Oh, Where Has My Little Dog Gone?"

Where, oh, where have my underwear gone?
Oh, where, oh, where could they be?
It's time for school, and my room is a mess.
Oh, where, oh, where could they be?

The school bus is here, and I've got to get dressed.
Oh, where, oh, where could they be?
I'll put on my pants, and I'll hope for the best,
and zip up my fly carefully.

Embarrassed

My zipper is broken.
There's bound to be jokin'
and normally I wouldn't care.
But today was the day,
I am sorry to say,
I didn't put on underwear.

Scary Costume

With an evil eye that can stop you cold,
and a bulbous warty nose,
a furrowed brow, a nasty scowl,
and old out-dated clothes,
my costume is the scariest
the world has ever seen.
I'm not an ogre, ghost, or ghoul,
I'm a teacher for Halloween.

A doctor with a needle.

A dentist with a drill.

The teacher in my classroom.

My little sister, Jill.

Standing under mistletoe.

The bully at my school.

My brother's dirty diaper.

A warm spot in the pool.

Looking up to see a seagull flying overhead.

After eating half a sandwich,
finding mold upon the bread.

27

On Halloween

On Halloween Frankenstein
     came to our door.
Mom didn't know he was real.

She gave him one gumball
     and not anymore.
Then Frankenstein said, "Here's the deal.

"I'm Frankenstein, ma'am,
     and I've come to this town
to be mean 'cause I'm in a bad mood.

"I'll scare you, then chase you,
     then tear your house down."
Mom scolded and said, "Don't be rude."

Then Frankenstein growled
     and said things that weren't kind,
so Mom grabbed a broom used for sweeping.

She swung with that broom
     to swat his behind,
and Frankenstein ran away weeping.

November 1st

Dial China on the phone.
Steal your brother's ice cream cone;
use the microwave to boil it.
Flush the car keys down the toilet.

Prance and dance. Skip and dip.
Tango, fandango, disco, flip.
Eat bananas. Eat the peels.
Bark like twenty singing seals.

Sing out silly, loud and long.
Sing a hard rock opera song.
To terrorize your dads and moms,
eat eighty super-sugar-bombs.

Ouch!

Meathead is our family dog.
Boy, he sure is dumb.
He never has retrieved a stick.
He hides when we yell, "Come."

Meathead is a friendly dog.
He plays with friends of mine.
Once when walking in the woods
we met a porcupine.

Meathead ran and wagged his tail,
off to make a friend.
I ran to try and stop him
'cause I knew how that would end.

I finally got between them,
and I hollered, "Meathead, sit!"
But Meathead charged full speed ahead,
he wasn't going to quit.

I raised my arms as Meathead jumped.
I wobbled when I caught him.
Then fell onto the porcupine,
and quills stuck in my bottom.

I've Been Working on My Homework

Sing to the tune of "I've Been Working on the Railroad"

I've been working on my homework
all the live long day.
I've been working on my homework
which I'd like to throw away.

What on earth's a preposition?
Seventeen multiplied by four?
Why's a platypus a mammal?
Can't take this no more!

Teacher, I don't know.
Wish that you would go,
and bother someone else today. I say,

teacher, I don't know.
Wish that you would go,
and bother someone else today.

Someone knows the capital of China.
Someone knows the answer,
        but I don't know. Oh —
Someone knows about the Forty-niners.
Someone does but I don't know. Oh, no.

A – E – I – O – U
A – E – I – O – U – O – U – Oh,
A – E – I – O – U
"Y" can be a vowel, too. It's true.

Room Cleaning Robot

Cleaning my bedroom is never much fun,
but my homework is lost, so it's gotta be done.
So, I'm building a robot to help clean my room
using junk on the floor like this moldy old spoon.
I'll build it with tee-shirts and three smelly socks,
four wrappers, a bag, and a cereal box,
a collection of worms that were dried in the sun,
my brother's rare comic, a cinnamon bun,
a library book that is way overdue,
a sneaker, a sandal, and Dad's missing shoe.
I'll keep on constructing with old underwear,
used tissues, dried spitballs, and fallen-out hair,
a half-eaten sandwich, that's half a year old,
a broken umbrella, I can't get to fold.
I'll top off my robot with the crushed soda cans,
a jar full of flies, and a shoe filled with sand.
As I finish my robot, I'm sad to confess,
my room is now clean, but my robot's a mess.

So Strong
I took them to the laundromat,
then washed them in the sink.
I've used those powders, sprays, and pads,
but still my sneakers stink.

Schoodic Point

Rainbows drift through sprays of mist
that blow from tops of swells.
As crests rise up then break and crash,
the buoys sound their bells.
Seagulls sit and ride the waves,
the ocean's rhythmic pulse.
Beneath the surf an ancient dance
of seaweeds, salt, and dulse.

Mucus Lament

I don't care much for handkerchiefs
and tissues are too flimsy.
I hate the prodding fingers
that come picking at their whimsy.
Eaters are disgusting.
Sleeves are used by losers.
I'd much prefer to stay right here
but boogers can't be choosers.

You Are My Behind

Sing to the tune of "You Are My Sunshine"

You are my behind,
my only behind.
You make me happy
when I must sit.
You'll never know, dear,
how much I love you.
Without you my pants wouldn't fit.

The other night, dear,
as I was sleeping,
I dreamed a nightmare —
that you were gone.
And what was worse, dear,
was when I realized
that my pants were not staying on.

You are my behind,
my only behind.
You make me happy
when I must sit.
You'll never know, dear,
how much I love you.
Without you my pants wouldn't fit.

When I awoke, dear,
I checked the mirror,
and I was glad that
I saw you there,
but just in case, dear,
you ever leave me,
I will buy suspenders to wear.

42

43

Little Miss Muffet
Traditional

Little Miss Muffet
sat on her tuffet
eating her curds and whey.
Along came a spider,
who sat down beside her
and frightened Miss Muffet away.

Little Miss Lou

Little Miss Lou
stepped in some poo
which was left by a dog on a walk.

When along came a skunk
who said that she stunk
Miss Lou exclaimed,
"You're one to talk!"

Going

To go
to Grandma's house
we drive a hundred miles.
We stop each time I yell, "I have
to go!"

Mistletoe Millie

The whole family's gathered,
and Mistletoe Millie
is kissing and smooching
and acting all silly.
She got Grampie Zeke
and kissed him on the cheek.
She caught Cousin Flynn
and kissed him on the chin.

She found Mr. Fips
and kissed him on the lips!
She ran up to me...
but I figured it out —
I held up our dog,
which she kissed on the snout.
She found it so gross
that she fell on the floor.
Guess she won't try
to kiss me anymore.

Our Dog

Our dog eats from the garbage can,
    and stirs up quite a stink.
Our dog eats from the garbage can,
    then goes to get a drink.
Our dog drinks from the toilet bowl,
    disgusting but it's true.
Our dog drinks from the toilet bowl,
    an awful thing to do.
Our dog's a very friendly dog,
    although he's kinda thick.
Our dog's a very friendly dog, but...
    his kisses make me sick.

The Prank

Two snacks upon the table,
one for Moxie, one for me.
I think it's time that I went on
a little eating spree.

I'll gobble hers, then swallow mine,
and it will make me glad
to be the one for a change,
making someone mad.

Chunky, crunchy, grainy, gritty,
a little hard to chew,
these snacks have made my breath smell like
a trash can or a shoe.

Moxie comes into the room.
I'm prepared if she attacks.
Instead, she laughs at me, and says,
"You just ate doggy snacks!"

Timbuktu

Slingshot

I'm gonna take a ride
on a slingshot made for two.
I'll be nice and take my sister.
We'll be flung to Timbuktu.

I'm gonna get back home
on a slingshot made for one.
With my sister stuck in Timbuktu
my life will be more fun.

I Think I'll Leave My Snowsuit On

Last night I didn't sleep so well.
I tossed and turned all night.
This morning I was snoring loud
and drooling, what a sight.
Woke up to see the bus outside
waiting in the snow.
My sister said, "Hey, snore-o-saur,
come on, it's time to go!"
Put on my snowsuit, boots, and hat
in a hurry-scurry dance.
Got to school, my face turned red,
I forgot to put on pants!

Be Glad You're Not a Knight

A knight dressed in armor
is never at ease
'cause it gets really gross
if he happens to sneeze.

And a bowl of baked beans
is a dangerous meal.
Passed gas can be deadly
to those dressed in steel.

And if you're embarrassed
by wetting the bed,
just imagine if you wet
your armor instead.

53

Haiku

Snow bending the boughs
finally falls from the tree
and lands on my face.

Why Do I Have to Learn to Count Money?

If you learn to count money before you get tall,
you can work in the ATM down at the mall.
The boy inside now is getting too large,
so learn to count quick and they'll put you in charge.
Listen to me 'cause I always know why.
I know it all, and, of course, I don't lie.

Humpty Dumpty
Traditional

Humpty Dumpty sat on a wall,
Humpty Dumpty had a great fall.
All the king's horses, and all the king's men,
couldn't put Humpty together again.

Humpty Dumpty

Humpty Dumpty sat in a lake.
He figured while floating he never would break.
But you know old Humpty, he had such bad luck.
The lightening came down, and old Humpty was struck.

57

Picture Day

My parents thought I should look nice. They dressed me in a gown.
But in a dress I get depressed, so all I did was frown.

FLASH

Mom thought a snack might make me smile. I had a lemon sucker.
When I was done my dad said, "Smile." All I could do was pucker.

FLASH

My father said, "Get this one right, or else I'll have you hung."
I thought the picture would look best if I stuck out my tongue.

FLASH

Next, they said to have a seat in the comfy chair,
On the way I scuffed my feet for spiky hair.

FLASH

When I made those faces, I meant it as a joke,
but now my father's really mad because the camera's broke.

Asymmetric Answers

'Twas noted by Miss Applebee,
who teaches us geometry,
my answers need less symmetry
with students sitting next to me.

How to Give Your Math Teacher a Really Bad Headache

My teacher asked what three plus two equals.
I said, "It depends on what you are adding.
If you add three kids and two ice cream cones,
you get two kids who need to wash their faces,
and one kid who is crying.

"Or, if you add three mice and two cats,
you get one cat that is full
and one cat that is very full.

"Or, if you add three apples and two oranges
you get..."

"Wait!" the teacher said, "You can't add apples and oranges."

"Sure you can," I said.

"If you add three apples and two oranges,
you get five fruit."

"Fine," my teacher said, "let's add three oranges and two oranges."

When I asked the teacher if she meant the fruit or the color,
I learned that more than one way to look at a question
equals one teacher
who needs two aspirin.

Jack and Jill

Traditional

Jack and Jill went up the hill,
to fetch a pail of water.
Jack fell down and broke his crown,
and Jill came tumbling after.

Jack and Jill

Jack and Jill sat on a hill
eating their curds and whey.
Till along came a Henny
whose last name was Penny.
She cried, "The sky's falling today!"

So they hid in a box till along came a fox.
He said, "You should follow my plan.
Come to my den,
little boy, girl, and hen.
You can hide with the Gingerbread Man!"

At the Farm

I heard a rabbit go, "Oink oink."
I heard a duck go, "Moo."
I heard a pig out in the mud
go, "Cock-a-doodle-doo."

I'm sure I heard the horses quack,
and then the roosters neigh.
"Old MacDonald Had a Farm"
was never sung this way.

The sounds these creatures ought to make
are taught in all the schools,
but disregard those lessons learned;
today is April Fool's!

What Really Happened to the Unicorns?

You know when Noah was a floatin' way out in the sea,
he was savin' all the creatures, so they could be free.
And here's a little somethin' that you may not have heard,
but my story is the truth, I give you my word.

Spend forty days at sea and you're bound to get thinner,
especially when raw fish is all you're havin' for dinner.
After thirty days of floatin' Noah said, "No more fish.
Tonight I'm gonna have me somethin' else on my dish."

So, Noah was a starvin' as he walked 'round the ship,
and gazed upon each creature with a smack of his lip.
He eyed a hog, a dog, a platypus, but sure as you're born,
the tastiest of them all was the Unicorn.

Thank You, Captain Cootie

Ripped my pants at school today
while going down the slide.
It wasn't just a little tear
I ripped 'em open wide.
Now all can see my Captain Cootie
purple underwear.
Although The Captain makes some laugh
I'm glad I've got him there.

Lesson Learned from Testing

I'm terrible at taking tests.
We have one everyday.
There are double tests in April
and triple tests in May.

We spend so much time taking tests;
there's little time to learn.
Instead of showing what we know,
it's more like crash and burn.

There's no time for experiments.
History's forgotten.
There's never time for poetry.
All these tests are rotten.

Geometry, geology,
civics, and fine arts
were taught to us in just one day.
The test has twenty parts!

Biology and physics
have been stuffed into my mind,
but all at such a rapid pace
I'm feeling left behind.

Today we read the dictionary.
Then we were assessed.
The only thing we learn at
school is how to take a test.

We're taught a lot of strategies
in hopes that we will pass
a test of what we haven't had
the time to learn in class.

I'm forming an opinion,
and I cannot seem to shake it.
It doesn't matter if you learn
as long as you can fake it.

Tomato Soup

When Meathead came into the house
we all yelled, "Oh, my gosh!"
Tomato soup soon filled the sink
to give our dog a wash.

He reeked like rotten sauerkraut,
mixed with moldy funk.
Meathead had been scented
by a smell-o-rific skunk.

After scrubbing Meathead clean
It seemed like such a waste
to let that soup go down the drain,
I thought, "How would it taste?"

Tomato soup is something
that my brother likes to eat.
So, I filled a bowl and placed it
on the table by his seat.

75

Why Does the Moon Follow Me?

The moon in the sky's out to getcha, ya know,
And that's why it follows wherever you go.
See, when you stand here at the edge of the park,
the moon up above watches you through the dark.

And now that we're home look up; there's the moon.
It's after you, Moxie, and may get you soon,
'cause the moon steals all children who don't behave well
and turns them to stars with a magical spell.

So keep one eye open, and don't snooze too deep;
the moon does it's work in the night when you sleep.
You know I'd protect you if only I could,
but the moon's sure to get you, unless you are good.

Listen to me 'cause I always know why.
I know it all, and, of course, I don't lie.

If we went crazy on this train,
then it would be a coo-coo train.

And if some flies filled up the train,
it would become a shoo-shoo train.

If Ballerinas rode the train,
then I'd call this a tutu train.

And if a cow came on the train,
why, we'd be on a moo-moo train.

Or if babies filled the train,
then this would be a goo-goo train.

And if we fell while on the train,
then we'd be on a boo-boo train.

But since we're eating on this train,
I guess it's just a chew-chew train.

Tomato Soup (A Second Helping)

When Murphy came into the house,
we all yelled, "Oh, my gosh!"
So, tomato soup soon filled the tub
to give that boy a wash.

He reeked like rotting garbage
filled with steaming sour gunk.
Murphy had been scented by
a smell-o-rific skunk.

Murphy soon was sitting,
soaking, naked in the tub.
Mom got a rag and plugged her nose,
then she began to scrub.

Tomato soup was in his hair
and getting in his eyes.
I thought, perhaps, Ol' Murph could use
a Moxie Day surprise.

Murphy was embarrassed.
I could not let him forget.
So, I took a picture, then I put it
on the Internet.

Mom!

Where's my Captain Cootie first edition comic book?
I've looked in every single place that's sensible to look.
I keep the comic hidden in the dresser with my socks,
sealed inside an acid-free, air-tight, cardboard box.
That comic never has been touched or seen the light of day.
Whoever took my comic book is gonna hafta pay.
I'll peek into my sister's room; she always takes my stuff.
But this is where I draw the line and say, "Enough's enough."
I hope that what I'm seeing's an illusion or mirage.
My sister cut The Captain out to use in her collage.

Magic Show

I'm going to a magic show.
There is a trick I hear they know.
So I'll go with my sister dear
and hope they make her disappear.

Funny Time

I went up to the rooftop. I brought the kitchen clock,
wound up like a pitcher and threw it 'cross the block.
Then I giggled, snickered, laughed, with Mama's watch in hand.
I threw that watch so forcefully; I bet it didn't land.
My mother doesn't seem to laugh. I don't know why she cries.
I heard her say, just yesterday, "It's funny how time flies."

We Could Have Bought a Hamster

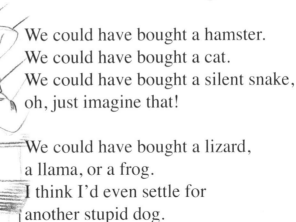

We could have bought a hamster.
We could have bought a cat.
We could have bought a silent snake,
oh, just imagine that!

We could have bought a lizard,
a llama, or a frog.
I think I'd even settle for
another stupid dog.

But someone said he knew a way
to fill our lives with joy.
He said, "Let's start a family
with a little girl and boy."

Now almost every single night
our home's filled with the sound
of screams and shouts and cries and pouts
that come from all around.

We could have bought a hamster.
We could have bought a cat.
We could have bought a silent snake,
oh, just imagine that!

Laughing

Giggle, giggle, snicker, laugh.
Giggle till you split in half.
Chortle-snort and chortle-roar;
laugh and roll around the floor.

Roll and rollick, jump for joy.
Hoot and holler, boy, oh, boy.
Laugh until you start to cry.
Laugh until you almost die.

Take a breath, then start again;
giggle till 'bout half past ten.
Laugh until you start to cough.
Laugh until your head falls off.

Laughing helps us to rejoice,
so laugh until you lose your voice.
Now you can't laugh anymore,
so sleep and make a silly snore.

Moxie Day and Family

DADDY DAY
will often say
a thing or two
that isn't true.

MAMA DAY
will often pray
for just one night
the kids won't fight.

MURPHY DAY
nothing goes his way.
A lucky charm
could cause him harm.

MEATHEAD
is well fed.
He runs like a flash
to eat from the trash.

Wiggledy Giggledy
Little Miss Moxie Day
pest to her teacher
and family but —

school kids all laugh at her
hyperhysterically
when she acts out like a
lunatic nut.

Poems with Moxie

Invite Robert to your school. Learn more at:

www.robertpottle.com

For podcasts and animations by

Robert Pottle visit:

www.lolpoetry.com